THE SECRET GARDEN OF YES AND NO

Lauraine Massamba

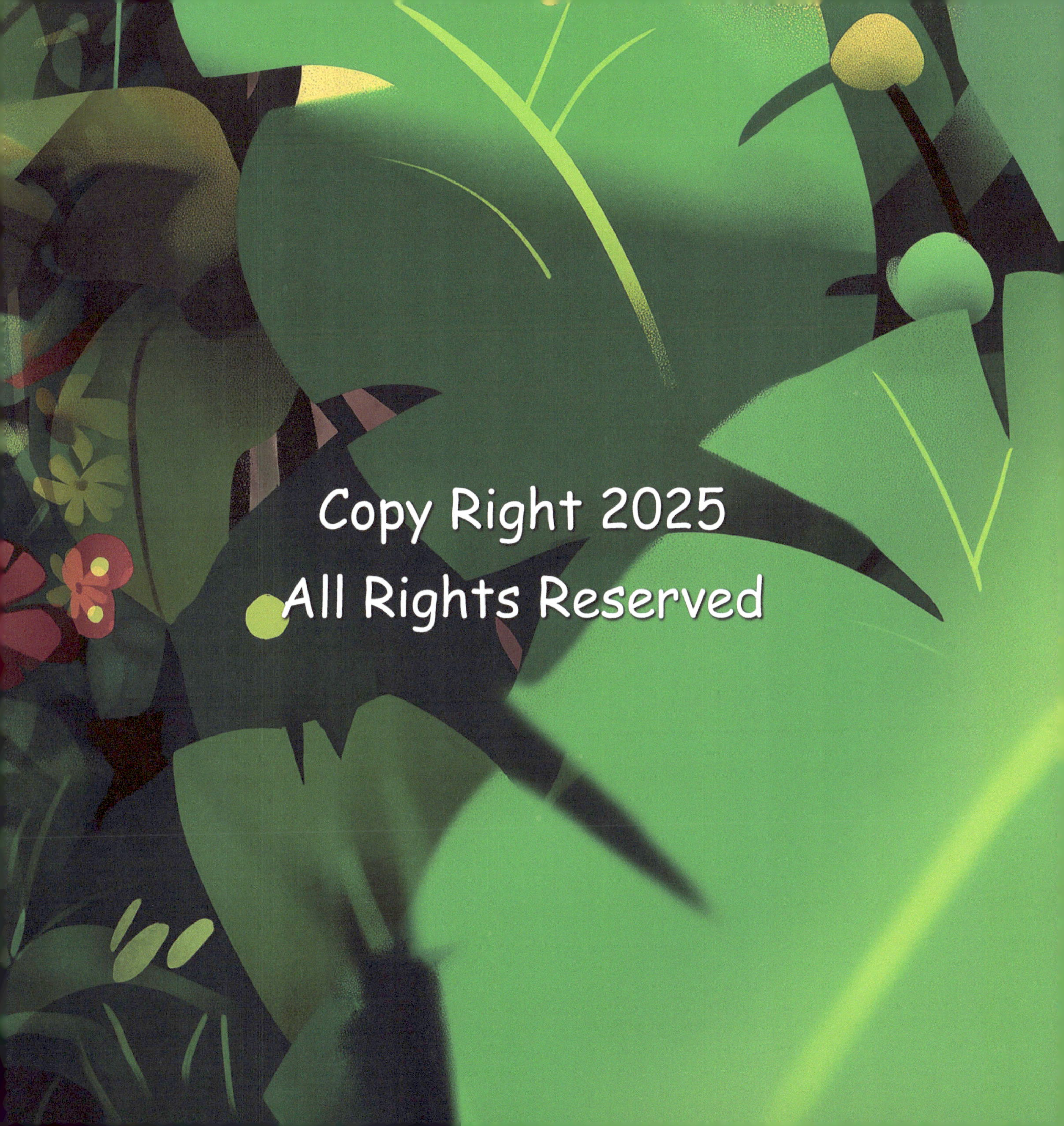

Before reading

Practising phonics and emotional awareness: Phase 2–3

- Read the book across multiple sessions to support understanding and fluency.
- Focus on key themes: feelings, personal space, yes/no choices, and asking for help.
- Encourage children to tap and read key words and phrases aloud.

Revisit and review: Pre-read

- Before reading the story, ask the child to:
  - Sound out these graphemes (GPCs)
  - Read the suggested words
  - Practice saying the helpful phrases in the story

Reading at home

This story helps your child understand their feelings and how to express them kindly and confidently. Encourage them to pause and reflect as they read. Ask: "What would you do in that part of the story?" If they get stuck, read it together and celebrate their effort!

Read the GPCs

sh   ch   th   ng   ck
ee   oo

Read the key words

yes   no   feel
safe   space
brave   help

Read the tricky words

you   my   to
the

Vocabulary – Ask & understand

feelings   boundaries
courage   trust
helper

Practise and apply: Read the book

- Tap-in and listen to your child read.
- Prompt them to use expressions when characters speak.
- Re-read favorite pages to boost fluency and confidence.

The Secret Garden of Yes and No

Learning to Protect Your Personal Space and Feelings

Lauraine Massamba

"Hello there, little one! Are you ready for a big adventure?" a soft voice says. "You're about to step into the Secret Garden of Yes and No. Here, every flower, bush, and tree has something special to share with you. Only you have the power to open the gate to this magical place!"

"I can do it!" says the child excitedly.

As you step onto the path, a gentle voice greets you, "Hello!" You look up to see an old oak tree with big, friendly eyes and a warm smile.

"Did you know everyone has feelings?" the tree says kindly. "Just like leaves changing colour, we all feel happy, sad, or even scared sometimes."

The tree stretches out a branch with a bright smile.. "What do you do when you feel happy?" it asks. "And how about when you feel sad?"

"I like dancing when I'm happy!" says the child. "And I hug my teddy if I'm sad."

The oak tree whispers, "It's okay to feel all kinds of feelings. They're like little messengers. They help you know when you feel safe and happy or when something feels wrong."
"Do you remember a time you felt very happy? Or maybe a time you felt a little scared?"

Just past the oak tree, you find a group of bushes that grow and shrink when you get close. "Hello there!" say the bushes in soft voices.

One bush explains, "We're here to show you personal space. Sometimes, it feels nice to be close to someone, but other times, you might want more space."

"If someone is too close, you can say, 'Please give me a little more space,'" another bush says with a friendly smile.

We're here to show you personal space," one bush explains. "Sometimes it's nice to be close, but other times you might want more space."
Another bush adds with a friendly smile, "If someone is too close, it's okay to say, 'Please give me a little more space.'"
The child practices, repeating, "Please give me more space," feeling stronger each time.

The child watches the bushes and repeats, "Please give me a little more space" and "It's okay if you come closer."
"You can always ask for more space if you need it, and other people can too," the bushes say kindly.

Next, you reach flowers divided into two sections: bright, gentle Yes Flowers, and strong, thorny No Flowers.

"Yes, please!" smile the Yes Flowers gently. "If you like something, say 'Yes, please!'"

"No, thank you," say the No Flowers firmly. "If something doesn't feel right, saying 'No' is honest and safe, not mean."

The child nods thoughtfully. "No means I'm honest and safe!" they say.

"Can you think of times you wanted to say 'Yes' or 'No'?" the flowers ask warmly.

The child confidently tries saying,
"Yes, please!" to the Yes Flowers and
"No, thank you!" to the No Flowers.
"Remember, you are the boss of your
Yes and No," repeat the flowers
cheerfully. "Always listen to what feels
right to you."
"I am the boss of my Yes and No!"
echoes the child proudly.

You follow the path to a sparkling river with rainbow-coloured water. "Welcome to the Rainbow River of Help!" says a wise fish.
"Helpers connect you to safety, just like this river connects the garden. Helpers are people you trust when something feels strange or wrong."
The fish explains, "Parents, teachers, and trusted family members can all be helpers."
"Like my mummy and my teacher!" smiles the child.

"If you ever feel worried, remember your helpers," says the fish kindly.
"They will always help you feel safe."
"Who are your helpers?" asks the fish gently.
"My family and my teachers," says the child, feeling calm and secure.

At the garden's end stands a tall tree covered in glowing golden keys. "These are Keys of Courage," says the tree proudly. "If you ever feel scared, keep one in your heart. It will help you be brave and talk to someone you trust."

The tree teaches a rhyme:

"If I feel strange, or something feels wrong,
I have a courage key to help me be strong.
I'll tell a trusted friend today,
So worries and fears can float away."

"I'll keep a courage key in my heart!" promises the child bravely.

Leaving the garden, you feel warm inside. The flowers, trees, and courage keys are now a part of you. Whenever needed, you can return to the Secret Garden of Yes and No, where strength and peace always await.

"Remember," whispers the garden as you close the gate, "You are the boss of your feelings and your space, and help is always here."

"I am the boss of my Yes and No!" the child repeats, smiling happily, holding the golden key close.

The Secret Garden of Yes and No

Learning to Protect Your Personal Space and Feelings

The Colouring Book

Lauraine Massamba

www.ingramcontent.com/pod-product-compliance
Lightning Source LLC
Chambersburg PA
CBHW042011080426
42734CB00002B/43